How to Be a Good Soccer Player

ID0980529

How to Be a Good Soccer Player

tips on kicking the ball,
heading and trapping,
and playing defense

by CLARE and FRANK GAULT
Illustrated by TONI GOFFE

SCHOLASTIC BOOK SERVICES
NEW YORK • TORONTO • LONDON • AUCKLAND • SYDNEY • TOKYO

ISBN: 0-590-31562-5

Text copyright © 1978 by Clare S. Gault and Frank M. Gault. Illustrations copyright © 1980 by Scholastic Magazines, Inc. Published by Scholastic Book Services, a division of Scholastic Magazines, Inc.

12 11 10 9 8 7 6 5 4   0 1 2 3 4 5/8

Printed in the U.S.A.   07

For the soccer players of
North Plainfield, New Jersey—
always among the best.

Contents

Soccer is the most popular team sport in the world. In most places it is called "football." That's natural, because in soccer the ball is kicked. In fact, no player except the goalkeeper may touch the ball with his hands.

It's hard to control a ball without using your hands. But it's the first thing you should learn. That's why this book is mostly tips about soccer skills, not about rules of the game. These tips are meant to help you to learn soccer faster — and have more fun while you're learning too.

Your equipment

All you need to play soccer are an open field and a ball. Almost any kind of ball will do. You can learn soccer skills with a regular soccer ball, a beach ball, a whiffle ball, even a tennis ball. When he was a small boy, the great soccer star Pelé learned to play with a sock stuffed with newspapers.

The important thing to learn is how to control a ball without using your hands. A small ball is good to practice with. You can carry it around in your pocket and practice anywhere you go.

What about other equipment? You could get regular soccer shoes. But you can also play in sneakers or street shoes. Some people even play barefoot if the field is soft enough.

Tips on kicking the ball

What is the best way to kick a soccer ball? You could kick it with your toes. This may be the way you think of first, but it's not the best way. Look at your foot. If you kick the ball with your toes, only a little bit of your shoe will hit the ball. This may not be enough to make the ball go where you want it to go.

Now look at your foot again. The top of your shoe is much wider than the toe.

 Kick the ball with the top of your foot, and you will be able to aim it much better. Your ankle and shin will help guide the ball too.

To kick the ball with the top of your foot, point your toes down just before you kick the ball. Your toes will slide under the ball and the top of your foot will hit the ball just below its center.

15

The long kick

Suppose you want to kick the ball far to reach a teammate way down the field. You need to make a long kick. Run up to the ball. Place one foot – your standing foot – a few inches to the side and a little behind the ball.

Lift your other leg – the kicking leg – and swing it way back. Bend your knee at the same time.

Now swing your kicking foot forward, toes pointed down. Lean backward. By doing this, you lift the ball into the air and send it far.

Be sure to let your leg continue going up after you have hit the ball. This is called "following through" – it is an important part of every kick.

Try this long kick on a ball that is standing still. Practice it with both your right and left foot. Kicking a ball back and forth with a friend is good practice and fun. Or, if you are alone, kick the ball up against a wall. Practice until you can make the ball go where you want it to go.

During a game, the ball may not be standing still. And you may want to make a long kick without stopping the ball first. It's much harder to kick a moving ball. You kick it about the same way, but you must hit the ball at exactly the right moment. How do you know when that right moment is? The only way to learn is by practicing.

Practice the kick on a ball moving straight toward you. Also, practice kicking a ball that is moving across your path. The more you practice, the better you will get. You will be able to kick the ball to a teammate far away.

The low, hard kick

Suppose you want the ball to stay low and move fast. This is the kind of kick you want when trying to get the ball into the goal.

Use the top of your foot so you can aim the ball well. Run up to the ball as you did for the long kick, but this time place your standing foot a few inches to the side and even with the ball, not behind it.

Again, swing your kicking leg back with the knee bent. Then swing your kicking leg forward, toes pointed down. Lean **forward** when you make this low, hard kick – not backward as you did for the long kick.

When you kick your foot forward, your knee will be over the ball and the top of your kicking foot will hit the ball in its center. This will make the ball go low, hard, and straight.

Remember to "follow through" after hitting the ball. Bring your kicking leg up and finish your kicking motion.

Practice the low, hard kick first when the ball is standing still. And be sure to practice it with both the right and left foot. After you think you can make the ball go where you want, practice with a ball that is moving toward you. And practice with a ball moving across your path.

Remember, it is the low, hard kick that usually scores goals.

The chip shot

Suppose you want to kick to a teammate not far from you, but there's a player from the other team in the way. You might want to pop the ball over the other player's head so he can't get it. Use a chip shot. The idea of the chip shot is to scoop up the ball with your foot and make it pop into the air.

Here's how to do it.

Move up to the ball as you did for the long kick. Place your standing foot a few inches to the side and a little behind the ball — but do not swing your kicking leg back. Just bend it at the knee. Lean backward a little and try to make your kicking foot just skim the ground so that your toes slip under the ball.

As you kick, lift your toes up.

Don't worry if you can't do the chip shot right away. It is a tough kick to learn. It takes lots of practice, but it's worth it. You can use this kick to score goals. If the goalkeeper comes out from the goal to block you, you may be able to pop the ball over his head and into the goal.

Kicking with the inside of your foot

If you only need to kick the ball a short distance, you may be able to control the ball best by using the inside of your foot.

This kick is not as fast or as hard as the low kick, but it is easier to aim the ball.

To kick with the inside of your foot, run up to the ball from the side. Place your standing foot a few inches away and even with the ball.

Turn the toes of your kicking foot out so that the side of your foot will strike the ball squarely. Swing your kicking leg back by twisting your body.

Swing your leg so that the inside of your foot strikes the ball just below its center. At this point, your kicking foot will be only a few inches off the ground.

Remember to "follow through."

At first, this kick may not seem natural. But you will find that you will be able to control the ball very well with a little practice. Of course, you should practice with both the right and left foot so that you can kick well from both sides.

Using the outside of your foot

Sometimes in a game you will want to make a quick kick to a teammate by using the outside of your foot. This kick is not powerful, but it can come in handy. The part of your foot to use is just below and in front of the ankle bone.

Run up to the ball. Place your standing foot a few inches away from and even with the ball.

Swing your kicking foot back. Just as you are about to strike the ball, turn your toes in and a little down. The outside of your foot should strike the ball just below its center and off to one side. This makes the ball jump to the side.

Dribbling

In soccer, dribbling is moving the ball with short kicks while keeping control of it. The ball is kicked with the toes – with the inside and outside of the foot.

When you are in the open and there are no players from the other team near you, you will be able to dribble the ball far ahead of you. You can run fast and you won't have to kick the ball often. But when a player from the other team comes near, you will want to keep the ball closer to you with short kicks.

Try to keep your body between the other player and the ball. This will make it harder for him to get it away from you.

Learning how to dribble and keep the ball under full control is hard. It takes plenty of practice. Try jogging slowly using both feet to do the kicking. Keep the ball close to you. Then start running fast and making longer kicks. Then slow down again and bring the ball under closer control. Keep changing your pace. Go up and down the field dribbling like this.

When you think you can control the ball well moving in a straight line, try zig-zagging with the ball. You and a friend can play a game of keep-away to see who can move the ball better and keep it longer.

Tips on heading
and trapping

As you know, you can't use your hands to touch the ball. What else can you do besides kicking it with your feet?

Heading the ball

You can use your head. This may sound funny, but the center of your forehead is very good for hitting and controlling a soccer ball. And it really doesn't hurt. Prove it to yourself by bouncing a ball off your forehead. See how long you can keep it in the air.

Plenty of goals are scored by heading. Suppose you are in front of the goal and a teammate kicks the ball to you high. You might not be able to use your feet to kick it, but you can use your forehead. Punch at the ball with your head. The best way is to get your whole body into the action. Jump off the ground to meet the ball and arch your back.

Now push your head out to strike the ball.

This is not as hard as it may sound. Hitting
the ball at the right moment is most important.
Have a friend throw a ball up for you and practice. See how well you can "head" it. Keep your
eyes open, if you can. You'll be able to aim the
ball much better.

Trapping the ball

Suppose the ball comes bouncing toward you and you want to wait for a teammate to get into position before you kick it. You will want to stop the ball first. You stop the ball by *trapping* it. Again – no hands!

If the ball is coming to you low, close to the ground, trap it with the bottom of your foot.

If the ball comes to you low and from an angle, trap it with the inside of your foot.

Or, you can trap the ball with the outside of your foot.

If the ball comes to you higher, you can stop it with the upper part of your leg. Raise your leg up and bend the knee. As the ball hits the upper part of your leg, pull your leg back and let the ball fall at your feet.

You can also use your chest or stomach to trap the ball. Let the ball hit you and just as it does, pull back and let the ball drop.

40

Tips on playing defense

In soccer, the ball moves up and down the field. One minute your team has the ball. The next minute the other team has it. When they do, you've got to get it back.

Being in position

When the other team has the ball, you know they will be trying to move it close to your goal. They will kick it back and forth to each other. Or, one of their players will dribble it.

When you are guarding a player who doesn't have the ball, make it hard for someone to kick it to him. Stay between your goal and the player you're guarding. But be ready to move in and get the ball if a kick isn't aimed just right. Keep your eyes on the ball. Then you will be able to see when it's coming in your direction.

When the player you're guarding has the ball, put pressure on him. Get in front of him. Make him try to get around you. The best way to stand is with your legs apart. Your weight is evenly balanced. You're ready to turn or jump in any direction.

It's a foul to charge into another player and knock him away from the ball. But you can kick at the ball or trap it with your feet. As the other player moves close, be ready to go for the ball.

You will have a good chance to get the ball if you keep after the dribbler. You might even force him to kick it to someone else. Then one of your teammates will have a chance to get the ball.

Goalkeeping

Each team has one goalkeeper. The goal-keeper is the only player who can use hands to touch the ball. If you are playing this position, use your hands to grab and hold the ball whenever possible.

If a ball comes to you close to the ground, get your body in front of the ball and cover it with your hands as fast as you can.

Do the same with a ball kicked higher.

Sometimes you may not be able to get your body in front of the ball. You may still be able to reach and grab it with your hands.

If the ball is too far away to catch, you can punch it with your fists. You can knock it wide of the goal.

The goalkeeper usually stays just in front of the goal, but there are times when he should come away from it.

Suppose the ball is bouncing loose in front of the goal. If you can get to the ball before a player from the other team, go out for it. Don't wait. Grab the ball and cover it with your hands.

Or suppose a player from the other team is dribbling toward your goal and is about to take a shot. You will often make it harder for him to take a good shot if you run out to meet him. Grab the ball with your hands if you can.

When you run out from the goal, your back will probably be turned to the goal. Here's a tip that may help you keep track of where you are. With your shoes, scuff a line in the grass directly in front of each goalpost. Then when you're out from your goal, you'll be able to tell where the posts are even when you can't see them.

When the action is in front of your goal, your teammates will be there helping defend it. They will probably have their backs to you. Let them know what they can do to help you. Shout to them, and keep on shouting: "George, watch out on the right side!" "Linda, cover the center – quick!"

Your teammates won't be able to watch what you're doing. They'll be too busy trying to get the ball. But they will be able to hear what you want them to do.

When you have grabbed the ball and smothered it, the ball is "dead." You have the free chance to put it back into play. The goalkeeper can throw it any way he likes, as he would a baseball, for instance. Or, he may kick it. Naturally, you'll want to get it to one of your teammates.

Tips on using your hands and arms

Throwing the ball in

There is one time you can use your hands on the ball during a soccer game even if you're not the goalkeeper. When the ball goes out of bounds on the side, it has to be thrown back into play. The rules say that both hands must be on the ball and both feet touching the ground. And the ball must be thrown over the head.

Put both hands on the ball. Spread your fingers wide. Your thumbs will almost touch at the back of the ball.

With your wrists, arms, and upper body, throw the ball. See how far you can throw it, how well you can aim it. Play catch with a friend, or throw the ball in this way up against a wall.

It's important to do it right, because a good throw-in can put your team in a better position to move the ball and to score.

There is another way you can use your arms and hands in soccer – for balance. Hold your arms out to your sides when kicking the ball.

Swing your arms to get more power when heading the ball.

Use your arms to keep your balance
on fast turns.

Keeping your balance is a key to being a good soccer player. Your arms and hands can help.

Soccer is a great game any boy or girl can play. You don't have to be big. You don't have to be tall. What you do have to know is how to make the ball behave. And that's something nearly everyone can learn – with practice.

Just dribbling a ball with your feet or kicking it up against a wall can be fun. Put up chalk marks. See how many times you can hit them. With a friend or two, play keep-away or have kicking contests.